Jean Walker

Dec. 1949.

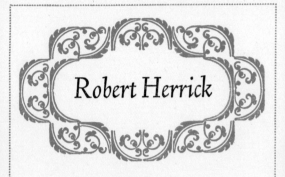

Robert Herrick

SONGS AND LYRICS

LOVE POEMS
NATURE · WINE · MIRTH
MORALITIES
HIMSELF & HIS BOOK
EPITAPHS

PETER PAUPER PRESS
MOUNT VERNON

AN INDEX OF FIRST LINES IS PRINTED
IN THE BACK OF THIS BOOK

THE ARGUMENT OF HIS BOOK

I SING of Brooks, of Blossomes, Birds, and Bowers:
Of April, May, of June, and July-Flowers.
I sing of May-poles, Hock-carts, Wassails, Wakes,
Of Bride-grooms, Brides, and of their Bridall-cakes.
I write of Youth, of Love, and have Accesse
By these, to sing of cleanly-Wantonnesse.
I sing of Dewes, of Raines, and piece by piece
Of Balme, of Oyle, of Spice, and Amber-Greece.
I sing of Times trans-shifting; and I write
How Roses first came Red, and Lillies White.
I write of Groves, of Twilights, and I sing
The Court of Mab, and of the Fairie-King.
I write of Hell; I sing (and ever shall)
Of Heaven, and hope to have it after all.

Love Poems

UPON LOVE

LOVE scorch'd my finger, but did spare
　　The burning of my heart:
To signifie, in Love my share
　　Sho'd be a little part.

Little I love; but if that he
　　Wo'd but that heat recall:
That joynt to ashes sho'd be burnt,
　　Ere I wo'd love at all.

❦

THE ROCK OF RUBIES: AND
THE QUARRIE OF PEARLS

SOME ask'd me where the Rubies grew?
　　And nothing I did say:
But with my finger pointed to
　　The lips of Julia.
Some ask'd how Pearls did grow, and where?
　　Then spoke I to my Girle,
To part her lips, and shew'd them there
　　The Quarelets of Pearl.

THE APRON OF FLOWERS

To gather Flowers Sappha went,
    And homeward she did bring
Within her Lawnie Continent,
    The treasure of the Spring.

She smiling blusht, and blushing smil'd,
    And sweetly blushing thus,
She lookt as she'd been got with child
    By young Favonius.

Her Apron gave (as she did passe)
    An Odor more divine,
More pleasing too, then ever was
    The lap of Proserpine.

❧

THE SHOOE TYING

Anthea bade me tye her shooe;
I did; and kist the Instep too:
And would have kist unto her knee,
Had not her Blush rebuked me.

❧

THE CARKANET

Instead of Orient Pearls of Jet,
I sent my Love a Carkanet.
About her spotlesse neck she knit
The lace, to honour me, or it:
Then think how wrapt was I to see
My Jet t'enthrall such Ivorie.

THE WEEPING CHERRY

I saw a Cherry weep, and why?
    Why wept it? but for shame,
Because my Julia's lip was by,
    And did out-red the same.
But pretty Fondling, let not fall
    A teare at all for that:
Which Rubies, Corralls, Scarlets, all
    For tincture, wonder at.

❧

UPON JULIA'S FALL

Julia was carelesse, and withall,
She rather took, then got a fall:
The wanton Ambler chanc'd to see
Part of her leggs sinceritie:
And ravish'd thus, It came to passe,
The Nagge (like to the Prophets Asse)
Began to speak, and would have been
A telling what rare sights h'ad seen:
And had told all; but did refraine,
Because his Tongue was ty'd againe.

❧

THE SCAR-FIRE

Water, water I desire,
Here's a house of flesh on fire:
Ope' the fountains and the springs,
And come all to Buckittings:
What ye cannot quench, pull downe;
Spoile a house, to save a towne:
Better tis that one shu'd fall,
Then by one, to hazard all.

ON HIMSELFE

Young I was, but now am old,
But I am not yet grown cold;
I can play, and I can twine
'Bout a Virgin like a Vine:
In her lap too I can lye
Melting, and in fancie die:
And return to life, if she
Claps my cheek, or kisseth me;
Thus, and thus it now appears
That our love out-lasts our yeeres.

KISSING USURIE

Biancha, Let
 Me pay the debt
I owe thee for a kisse
 Thou lend'st to me;
 And I to thee
Will render ten for this:

 If thou wilt say,
 Ten will not pay
For that so rich a one;
 Ile cleare the summe,
 If it will come
Unto a Million.

 By this I guesse,
 Of happinesse
Who has a little measure:
 He must of right,
 To th'utmost mite,
Make payment for his pleasure.

UPON THE LOSSE OF
HIS MISTRESSES

I HAVE lost, and lately, these
Many dainty Mistresses:
Stately Julia, prime of all;
Sapho next, a principall:
Smooth Anthea, for a skin
White, and Heaven-like Chrystalline:
Sweet Electra, and the choice
Myrha, for the Lute, and Voice.
Next, Corinna, for her wit,
And for the graceful use of it:
With Perilla: All are gone;
Onely Herrick's left alone,
For to number sorrow by
Their departures hence, and die.

TO HIS MISTRESSE

CHOOSE me your Valentine;
    Next, let us marry:
Love to the death will pine,
    If we long tarry.

Promise, and keep your vowes,
    Or vow ye never:
Loves doctrine disallowes
    Troth-breakers ever.

You have broke promise twice
    (Deare) to undoe me;
If you prove faithlesse thrice,
    None then will wooe ye.

ONE ask'd me where the Roses grew?
  I bade him not goe seek;
But forthwith bade my Julia shew
  A bud in either cheek.

I CALL AND I CALL

I CALL, I call, who doe ye call?
The Maids to catch this Cowslip-ball:
But since these Cowslips fading be,
Troth, leave the flowers, and Maids, take me.
Yet, if that neither you will doe,
Speak but the word, and Ile take you.

DELIGHT IN DISORDER

A SWEET disorder in the dresse
Kindles in cloathes a wantonnesse:
A Lawne about the shoulders thrown
Into a fine distraction:
An erring Lace, which here and there
Enthralls the Crimson Stomacher:
A Cuffe neglectfull, and thereby
Ribbands to flow confusedly:
A winning wave (deserving Note)
In the temptestuous petticote:
A carelesse shooe-string, in whose tye
I see a wilde civility:
Doe more bewitch me, then when Art
Is too precise in every part.

10

JULIA, I bring
To thee this Ring,
Made for thy finger fit;
To shew by this,
That our love is
(Or sho'd be) like to it.

Close though it be,
The joynt is free:
So when Love's yoke is on,
It must not gall,
Or fret at all,
With hard oppression.

But it must play
Still either way;
And be, too, such a yoke,
As not too wide,
To over-slide;
Or be so strait to choak.

So we, who beare,
This beame, must reare
Our selves to such a height:
As that the stay
Of either may
Create the burden light.

And as this round
Is no where found
To flaw, or else to sever:
So let our love
As endless prove;
And pure as Gold for ever.

WATER, Water I espie:
Come, and coole ye; all who frie
In your loves; but none as I.

Though a thousand showres be
Still a falling, yet I see
Not one drop to light on me.

Happy you, who can have seas
For to quench ye, or some ease
From your kinder Mistresses.

I have one, and she alone,
Of a thousand thousand known,
Dead to all compassion.

Such an one, as will repeat
Both the cause, and make the heat
More by Provocation great.

Gentle friends, though I despaire
Of my cure, doe you beware
Of those Girles, which cruell are.

ON HIMSELFE

LOVE-SICK I am, and must endure
A desp'rate grief, that finds no cure.
Ah me! I try; and trying, prove,
No Herbs have power to cure Love.
Only one Soveraign salve, I know,
And that is Death, the end of Woe.

WHEN I thy singing next shall heare,
Ile wish I might turne all to eare,
To drink in Notes, and Numbers; such
As blessed soules cann't heare too much:
Then melted down, there let me lye
Entranc'd, and lost confusedly:
And by thy Musique strucken mute,
Die, and be turn'd into a Lute.

❧

THE VISION

SITTING alone (as one forsook)
Close by a Silver-shedding Brook;
With hands held up to Love, I wept;
And after sorrowes spent, I slept:
Then in a Vision I did see
A glorious forme appeare to me:
A Virgins face she had; her dresse
Was like a sprightly Spartanesse.
A silver bow with green silk strung,
Down from her comely shoulders hung:
And as she stood, the wanton Aire
Dandled the ringlets of her haire.
Her legs were such Diana shows,
When tuckt up she a hunting goes;
With Buskins shortened to descrie
The happy dawning of her thigh:
Which when I saw, I made accesse
To kisse that tempting nakednesse:
But she forbade me, with a wand
Of Mirtle she had in her hand:
And chiding me, said, Hence, Remove,
Herrick, thou art too coorse to love.

CUPID as he lay among
Roses, by a Bee was stung.
Whereupon in anger flying
To his Mother, said thus crying;
Help! O help! your Boy's a dying.
And why, my pretty Lad, said she?
Then blubbering, replyed he,
A winged Snake has bitten me,
Which Country people call a Bee.
At which she smil'd; then with her hairs
And kisses drying up his tears:
Alas! said she, my Wag! if this
Such a pernicious torment is:
Come tel me then, how great's the smart
Of those, thou woundest with thy Dart!

DISSWASIONS FROM IDLENESSE

CYNTHIUS pluck ye by the eare,
That ye may good doctrine heare.
Play not with the maiden-haire;
For each Ringlet there's a snare.
Cheek, and eye, and lip, and chin;
These are traps to take fooles in.
Armes, and hands, and all parts else,
Are but Toiles, or Manicles
Set on purpose to enthrall
Men, but Slothfulls most of all.
Live employ'd, and so live free
From these fetters; like to me
Who have found, and still can prove,
The lazie man the most doth love.

14

THE FROZEN ZONE: OR,
JULIA DISDAINFULL

WHITHER? Say, whither shall I fly,
To slack these flames wherein I frie?
To the Treasures, shall I goe,
Of the Raine, Frost, Haile, and Snow?
Shall I search the under-ground,
Where all Damps, and Mists are found?
Shall I seek (for speedy ease)
All the floods, and frozen seas?
Or descend into the deep,
Where eternall cold does keep?
These may coole; but there's a Zone
Colder yet then any one:
That's my Julia's breast; where dwels
Such destructive Ysicles;
As that the Congelation will
Me sooner starve, then those can kill.

❧

UPON JULIA'S RECOVERY

DROOP, droop no more, or hang the head
Ye Roses almost withered;
Now strength, and newer Purple get,
Each here declining Violet.
O Primroses! let this day be
A Resurrection unto ye;
And to all flowers ally'd in blood,
Or sworn to that sweet Sister-hood:
For Health on Julia's cheek hath shed
Clarret, and Creame commingled.
And those her lips doe now appeare
As beames of Corrall, but more cleare.

UPON ROSES

UNDER a Lawne, then skyes more cleare,
Some ruffled Roses nestling were:
And snugging there, they seem'd to lye
As in a flowrie Nunnery:
They blush'd, and look'd more fresh then flowers
Quickned of late by Pearly showers:
And all, because they were possest
But of the heat of Julia's breast:
Which as a warme, and moistned spring,
Gave them their ever flourishing.

TO PERENNA

WHEN I thy Parts runne o're, I can't espie
In any one, the least indecencie:
But every Line, and Limb diffused thence,
A faire, and unfamiliar excellence:
So, that the more I look, the more I prove,
Ther's still more cause, why I the more should love.

LOVE'S PLAY AT PUSH-PIN

LOVE and my selfe (beleeve me) on a day
At childish Push-pin (for our sport) did play:
I put, he pusht, and heedless of my skin,
Love prickt my finger with a golden pin:
Since which, it festers so, that I can prove
'Twas but a trick to poyson me with love:
Little the wound was; greater was the smart,
The finger bled, but burnt was all my heart.

Make me a heaven; and make me there
Many a lesse and greater spheare.
Make me the straight, and oblique lines;
The Motions, Lations, and the Signes.
Make me a Chariot, and a Sun;
And let them through a Zodiac run:
Next, place me Zones, and Tropicks there;
With all the Seasons of the Yeare.
Make me a Sun-set; and a Night:
And then present the Mornings-light
Cloath'd in her Chamlets of Delight.
To these, make Clouds to poure downe raine;
With weather foule, then faire againe.
And when, wise Artist, that thou hast,
With all that can be, this heaven grac't;
Ah! what is then this curious skie,
But onely my Corinna's eye?

TO DEWES. A SONG

I burn, I burn; and beg of you
To quench, or coole me with your Dew.
I frie in fire, and so consume,
Although the Pile be all perfume.
Alas! the heat and death's the same;
Whether by choice, or common flame:
To be in Oyle of Roses drown'd,
Or water; where's the comfort found?
Both bring one death; and I die here,
Unlesse you coole me with a Teare:
Alas! I call; but ah! I see
Ye coole, and comfort all, but me.

TO ELECTRA

MORE white then whitest Lillies far,
Or Snow, or whitest Swans you are:
More white then are the whitest Creames,
Or Moone-light tinselling the streames:
More white then Pearls, or Juno's thigh;
Or Pelops Arme of Yvorie.
True, I confesse; such Whites as these
May me delight, not fully please:
Till, like Ivion's Cloud you be
White, warme, and soft to lye with me.

❧

TO THE VIRGINS, TO MAKE MUCH OF TIME

GATHER ye Rose-buds while ye may,
    Old Time is still a flying:
And this same flower that smiles to day,
    To morrow will be dying.

The glorious Lamp of Heaven, the Sun,
    The higher he's a getting;
The sooner will his Race be run,
    And neerer he's to Setting.

That Age is best, which is the first,
    When Youth and Blood are warmer;
But being spent, the worse, and worst
    Times, still succeed the former.

Then be not coy, but use your time;
    And while ye may, goe marry:
For having lost but once your prime,
    You may for ever tarry.

THE BLEEDING HAND: OR,
THE SPRIG OF EGLANTINE

FROM this bleeding hand of mine,
Take this sprig of Eglantine,
Which (though sweet unto your smell)
Yet the fretfull bryar will tell,
He who plucks the sweets shall prove
Many thorns to be in Love.

❧

JULIA'S PETTICOAT

THY Azure Robe, I did behold,
As ayrie as the leaves of gold;
Which erring here, and wandring there,
Pleas'd with transgression ev'ry where:
Sometimes 'two'd pant, and sigh, and heave,
As if to stir it scarce had leave:
But having got it; thereupon,
'Two'd make a brave expansion.
And pounc't with Stars, it shew'd to me
Like a Celestiall Canopie.
Sometimes 'two'd blaze, and then abate,
Like to a flame growne moderate:
Sometimes away 'two'd wildly fling;
Then to thy thighs so closely cling,
That some conceit did melt me downe,
As Lovers fall into a swoone:
And all confus'd, I there did lie
Drown'd in Delights; but co'd not die.
That Leading Cloud, I follow'd still,
Hoping t'ave seene of it my fill;
But ah! I co'd not: sho'd it move
To Life Eternal, I co'd love.

So look the mornings when the Sun
Paints them with fresh Vermilion:
So Cherries blush, and Kathern Peares,
And Apricocks, in youthful yeares:
So Corrolls looke more lovely Red,
And Rubies lately polished:
So purest Diaper doth shine,
Stain'd by the Beames of Clarret wine:
As Julia looks when she doth dress
Her either cheeke with bashfullness.

CHERRIE-RIPE

CHERRIE-RIPE, Ripe, Ripe, I cry,
Full and faire ones; come and buy:
If so be, you ask me where
They doe grow? I answer, There,
Where my Julia's lips doe smile;
There's the Land, or Cherry-Ile:
Whose Plantations fully show
All the yeere, where Cherries grow.

TO CARNATIONS. A SONG

STAY while ye will, or goe;
    And leave no scent behind ye:
Yet trust me, I shall know
    The place, where I may find ye.

Within my Lucia's cheek,
    (Whose Livery ye weare)
Play ye at Hide or Seek,
    I'm sure to find ye there.

My faithful friend, if you can see
The Fruit to grow up, or the Tree:
If you can see the colour come
Into the blushing Peare, or Plum:
If you can see the water grow
To cakes of Ice, or flakes of Snow:
If you can see, that drop of raine
Lost in the wild sea, once againe:
If you can see, how Dreams do creep
Into the Brain by easie sleep:
Then there is hope that you may see
Her love me once, who now hates me.

NOT TO LOVE

He that will not love, must be
My Scholar, and learn this of me:
There be in Love as many feares,
As the Summers Corne has eares:
Sighs, and sobs, and sorrowes more
Then the sand, that makes the shore:
Freezing cold, and firie heats,
Fainting swoones, and deadly sweats;
Now an Ague, then a Fever,
Both tormenting Lovers ever.
Wods't thou know, besides all these,
How hard a woman 'tis to please?
How crosse, how sullen, and how soone
She shifts and changes like the Moone.
How false, how hollow she's in heart;
And how she is her owne least part:
How high she's priz'd, and worth but small;
Little thou'd love, or not at all.

As Julia once a-slumb'ring lay,
It chanc't a Bee did flie that way,
(After a dew, or dew-like shower)
To tipple freely in a flower.
For some rich flower, he took the lip
Of Julia and began to sip;
But when he felt he suckt from thence
Hony, and in the quintessence:
He drank so much he scarce co'd stir;
So Julia took the Pilferer.
And thus surpriz'd (as Filchers use)
He thus began himselfe t'excuse:
Sweet Lady-Flower, I never brought
Hither the least one theeving thought:
But taking those rare lips of yours
For some fresh, fragrant, luscious flowers:
I thought I might there take a taste,
Where so much sirrop ran at waste.
Besides, know this, I never sting
The flower that gives me nourishing:
But with a kisse, or thanks, doe pay
For Honie, that I beare away.
This said, he laid his little scrip
Of hony, 'fore her Ladiship:
And told her, (as some tears did fall)
That, that he took, and that was all.
At which she smil'd; and bade him goe
And take his bag; but thus much know,
When next he came a pilfring so,
He sho'd from her full lips derive,
Hony enough to fill his hive.

TO LOVE

I'm free from thee; and thou no more shalt heare
My puling Pipe to beat against thine eare:
Farewell my shackles, (though of pearle they be)
Such precious thraldome ne'r shall fetter me.
He loves his bonds, who when the first are broke,
Submits his neck unto a second yoke.

~

TO SILVIA TO WED

Let us (though late) at last (my Silvia) wed;
And loving lie in one devoted bed.
Thy Watch may stand, my minutes fly poste haste;
No sound calls back the yeere that once is past.
Then sweetest Silvia, let's no longer stay;
True love, we know, precipitates delay.
Away with doubts, all scruples hence remove;
No man at one time, can be wise, and love.

~

THE SADNESS OF THINGS
FOR SAPHO'S SICKNESSE

Lillies will languish; Violets look ill;
Sickly the Prim-rose: Pale the Daffadill:
That gallant Tulip will hang down his head,
Like to a Virgin newly ravished.
Pansies will weep; and Marygolds will wither;
And keep a Fast, and Funerall together,
If Sapho droop; Daisies will open never,
But bid Good-night, and close their lids for ever.

23

UPON HIS JULIA

WILL ye heare, what I can say
Briefly of my Julia?
Black and rowling is her eye,
Double chinn'd, and forehead high:
Lips she has, all Rubie red,
Cheeks like Creame Enclarited:
And a nose that is the grace
And Proscenium of her face.
So that we may guesse by these,
The other parts will richly please.

THE POMANDER BRACELET

To me my Julia lately sent
A Bracelet richly Redolent:
The Beads I kist, but most lov'd her
That did perfume the Pomander.

THE VISION TO ELECTRA

I DREAM'D we both were in a bed
Of Roses, almost smothered:
The warmth and sweetness had me there
Made lovingly familiar:
But that I heard thy sweet breath say,
Faults done by night, will blush by day:
I kist thee (panting), and I call
Night to the Record; that was all.
But ah! if empty dreames so please,
Love give me more such nights as these.

GOOD morrow to the Day so fair;
   Good morning Sir to you:
Good morrow to mine own torn hair
   Bedabled with the dew.

Good morning to this Prim-rose too;
   Good morrow to each maid;
That will with flowers the Tomb bestrew,
   Wherein my Love is laid.

Ah woe is me, woe, woe is me,
   Alack and welladay!
For pitty, Sir, find out that Bee,
   Which bore my Love away.

I'le seek him in your Bonnet brave;
   Ile seek him in your eyes;
Nay, now I think th'ave made his grave
   I'th'bed of strawburies.

Ile seek him there; I know, ere this,
   The cold, cold Earth doth shake him;
But I will go, or send a kisse
   By you, Sir, to awake him.

Pray hurt him not; though he be dead,
   He knowes well who do love him,
And who with green-turfes reare his head,
   And who do rudely move him.

He's soft and tender (Pray take heed)
   With bands of Cow-slips bind him;
And bring him home, but 'tis decreed,
   That I shall never find him.

BID me to live, and I will live
  Thy Protestant to be:
Or bid me love, and I will give
  A loving heart to thee.

A heart as soft, a heart as kind,
  A heart as sound and free,
As in the whole world thou canst find,
  That heart Ile give to thee.

Bid that heart stay, and it will stay,
  To honour thy Decree:
Or bid it languish quite away,
  And't shall doe so for thee.

Bid me to weep, and I will weep,
  While I have eyes to see:
And having none, yet I will keep
  A heart to weep for thee.

Bid me despaire, and Ile despaire,
  Under that Cypresse tree:
Or bid me die, and I will dare
  E'en Death, to die for thee.

Thou art my life, my love, my heart,
  The very eyes of me:
And hast command of every part,
  To live and die for thee.

HER BED

SEE'ST thou that Cloud as silver cleare,
Plump, soft & swelling every where?
Tis Julia's Bed, and she sleeps there.

UPON JULIA'S CLOTHES

WHEN as in silks my Julia goes,
Then, then (me thinks) how sweetly flowes
That liquefaction of her clothes.

Next, when I cast mine eyes and see
That brave Vibration each way free;
O how that glittering taketh me!

❧

TO SPRINGS AND FOUNTAINS

I HEARD ye co'd coole heat; and came
With hope you would allay the same:
Thrice I have washt, but feel no cold,
Nor find that true, which was foretold.
Me thinks like mine, your pulses beat;
And labour with unequall heat:
Cure, cure your selves, for I discrie,
Ye boil with Love, as well as I.

❧

LOVE PERFUMES ALL PARTS

IF I kisse Anthea's brest,
There I smell the Phenix nest:
If her lip, the most sincere
Altar of Incense, I smell there.
Hands, and thighs, and legs, are all
Richly Aromaticall.
Goddesse Isis cann't transfer
Musks and Ambers more from her:
Nor can Juno sweeter be,
When she lyes with Jove, then she.

27

I COULD wish you all, who love,
That ye could your thoughts remove
From your Mistresses, and be,
Wisely wanton (like to me.)
I could wish you dispossest
Of that *Fiend that marres your rest,*
And with Tapers comes to fright
Your weake senses in the night.
I co'd wish, ye all, who frie
Cold as Ice, or coole as I.
But if flames best like ye, then
Much good do't ye Gentlemen.
I a merry heart will keep,
While you wring your hands and weep.

TO THE ROSE. SONG

GOE happy Rose, and enterwove
With other Flowers, bind my Love.
  Tell her too, she must not be,
  Longer flowing, longer free,
  That so oft has fetter'd me.

Say (if she's fretful) I have bands
Of Pearle, and Gold, to bind her hands:
  Tell her, if she struggle still,
  I have Mirtle rods, (at will)
  For to tame, though not to kill.

Take thou my blessing, thus, and goe,
And tell her this, but doe not so,
  Lest a handsome anger flye,
  Light a Lightning, from her eye,
  And burn thee up, as well as I.

A WILLOW Garland thou did'st send
   Perfum'd (last day) to me:
Which did but only this portend,
   I was forsook by thee.

Since so it is; Ile tell thee what,
   To morrow thou shalt see
Me weare the Willow; after that,
   To dye upon the Tree.

As Beasts unto the Altars go
   With Garlands drest, so I
Will with my Willow-wreath also,
   Come forth and sweetly dye.

                   ⤙❧

TO OENONE

WHAT Conscience, say, is it in thee
   When I a Heart had one,
To take away that Heart from me,
   And to retain thy own?

For shame or pitty now encline
   To play a loving part;
Either to send me kindly thine,
   Or give me back my heart.

Covet not both; but if thou dost
   Resolve to part with neither;
Why! yet to shew that thou art just,
   Take me and mine together.

29

TO DIANEME

Sweet, be not proud of those two eyes,
Which Star-like sparkle in their skies:
Nor be you proud, that you can see
All hearts your captives; yours, yet free:
Be you not proud of that rich haire,
Which wantons with the Love-sick aire:
When as that Rubie, which you weare,
Sunk from the tip of your soft eare,
Will last to be a precious Stone,
When all your world of Beautie's gone.

TO ELECTRA

'Tis Ev'ning, my Sweet,
And dark; let us meet;
Long time w'ave here been a toying:
And never, as yet,
That season co'd get,
Wherein t'ave had an enjoying.

For pity or shame,
Then let not Love's flame,
Be ever and ever a spending;
Since now to the Port
The path is but short;
And yet our way has no ending.

Time flyes away fast;
Our houres doe waste:
The while we never remember,
How soone our life, here,
Growes old with the yeere,
That dyes with the next December.

UPON SAPHO, SWEETLY PLAYING

WHEN thou do'st play, and sweetly sing,
Whether it be the voice or string,
Or both of them, that do agree
Thus to en-trance and ravish me:
This, this I know, I'm oft struck mute;
And dye away upon thy Lute.

❧

CLOTHES DO BUT CHEAT
AND COUSEN US

AWAY with silks, away with Lawn,
Ile have no Sceans, or Curtains drawn:
Give me my Mistresse, as she is,
Drest in her nak't simplicities:
For as my Heart, ene so mine Eye
Is won with flesh, not Drapery.

❧

UPON A BLACK TWIST,
ROUNDING HER ARM

I SAW about her spotlesse wrist,
Of blackest silk, a curious twist;
Which, circumvolving gently, there
Enthrall'd her Arme, as Prisoner.
Dark was the Jayle; but as if light
Had met t'engender with the night;
Or so, as Darknesse made a stay
To shew at once, both night and day.
One fancie more! but if there be
Such Freedome in Captivity;
I beg of Love, that ever I
May in like Chains of Darknesse lie.

UPON LOVE

I HELD Love's head while it did ake;
    But so it chanc't to be;
The cruell paine did his forsake,
    And forthwith came to me.

Ai me! How shal my griefe be stil'd?
    Or where else shall we find
One like to me, who must be kill'd
    For being too-too-kind?

❧

UPON LOVE

I PLAID with Love, as with the fire
    The wanton Satyre did;
Nor did I know, or co'd descry
    What under there was hid.

That Satyre he but burnt his lips;
    (But mine's the greater smart)
For kissing Love's dissembling chips,
    The fire scorcht my heart.

❧

LOVE LIGHTLY PLEASED

LET faire or foule my Mistresse be,
Or low, or tall, she pleaseth me:
Or let her walk, or stand, or sit,
The posture hers, I'm pleas'd with it.
Or let her tongue be still, or stir,
Gracefull is ev'ry thing from her.
Or let her Grant, or else Deny,
My Love will fit each Historie.

When I behold a Forrest spread
With silken trees upon thy head;
And when I see that other Dresse
Of flowers set in comlinesse:
When I behold another grace
In the ascent of curious Lace,
Which like a Pinacle doth shew
The top, and the top-gallant too.
Then, when I see thy Tresses bound
Into an Ovall, square, or round;
And knit in knots far more then I
Can tell by tongue; or true-love tie:
Next, when those Lawnie Filmes I see
Play with a wild civility:
And all those airie silks to flow,
Alluring me, and tempting so:
I must confesse mine eye and heart
Dotes less on Nature, then on Art.

TO SYCAMORES

I'm sick of Love; O let me lie
Under your shades, to sleep or die!
Either is welcome; so I have
Or here my Bed, or here my Grave.
Why do you sigh, and sob, and keep
Time with the tears, that I do weep?
Say, have ye sence, or do you prove
What Crucifixions are in Love?
I know ye do; and that's the why,
You sigh for Love, as wel as I.

WHAT I fancy, I approve,
No Dislike there is in love:
Be my Mistresse short or tall,
And distorted there-withall:
Be she likewise one of those,
That an Acre hath of Nose:
Be her forehead, and her eyes
Full of incongruities:
Be her cheeks so shallow too,
As to shew her Tongue wag through:
Be her lips ill hung, or set,
And her grinders black as jet;
Ha's she thinne haire, hath she none,
She's to me a Paragon.

IN PRAISE OF WOMEN

O JUPITER, sho'd I speake ill
Of woman-kind, first die I will;
Since that I know, 'mong all the rest
Of creatures, woman is the best.

CHOP-CHERRY

THOU gav'st me leave to kisse;
Thou gav'st me leave to wooe;
Thou mad'st me thinke by this,
And that, thou lov'dst me too.

But I shall ne'r forget,
How for to make thee merry;
Thou mad'st me chop, but yet,
Another snapt the Cherry.

34

HER Eyes the Glow-worme lend thee,
The Shooting Starres attend thee
 And the Elves also,
 Whose little eyes glow,
Like the sparks of fire, befriend thee.

No Will-o'th'-Wispe mis-light thee;
Nor Snake, or Slow-worme bite thee:
 But on, on thy way
 Not making a stay,
Since Ghost ther's none to affright thee.

Let not the darke thee cumber;
What though the Moon do's slumber?
 The Starres of the night
 Will lend thee their light,
Like Tapers cleare without number.

Then Julia let me wooe thee,
Thus, thus to come unto me:
 And when I shall meet
 Thy silv'ry feet,
My soule Ile poure into thee.

     ❧

LUCIA DABLED IN THE DEAW

MY Lucia in the deaw did go,
And prettily bedabled so,
Her cloaths held up, she shew'd withall
Her decent legs, cleane, long and small.
I follow'd after to descrie
Part of the nak't sincerity;
But still the envious Scene between
Deni'd the Mask I wo'd have seen.

A CHRISTALL Violl Cupid brought,
　　Which had a juice in it:
Of which who drank, he said no thought
　　Of Love he sho'd admit.

I greedy of the prize, did drinke,
　　And emptied soon the glasse;
Which burnt me so, that I do thinke
　　The fire of hell it was.

Give me my earthen Cups again,
　　The Christall I contemne;
Which, though enchas'd with Pearls, contain
　　A deadly draught in them.

And thou O Cupid! come not to
　　My Threshold, since I see,
For all I have, or else can do,
　　Thou still wilt cozen me.

TO ELECTRA

ILE come to thee in all those shapes
As Jove did, when he made his rapes:
Onely, Ile not appeare to thee,
As he did once to Semele.
Thunder and Lightning Ile lay by,
To talk with thee familiarly.
Which done, then quickly we'll undresse
To one and th'others nakednesse.
And ravisht, plunge into the bed,
(Bodies and souls commingled)
And kissing, so as none may heare,
We'll weary all the Fables there.

LOVE DISLIKES NOTHING

WHATSOEVER thing I see,
Rich or poore although it be;
'Tis a Mistresse unto mee.

Be my Girle, or faire or browne,
Do's she smile, or do's she frowne:
Still I write a Sweet-heart downe.

Be she rough, or smooth of skin;
When I touch, I then begin
For to let Affection in.

Be she bald, or do's she weare
Locks incurl'd of other haire;
I shall find enchantment there.

Be she whole, or be she rent,
So my fancie be content,
She's to me most excellent.

Be she fat, or be she leane,
Be she sluttish, be she cleane,
I'm a man for ev'ry Sceane.

❧

A HYMNE TO VENUS

SEA-BORN Goddesse, let me be,
By thy sonne thus grac't, and thee;
That when ere I wooe, I find
Virgins coy, but not unkind.
Let me when I kisse a maid,
Taste her lips, so over-laid
With Loves-sirrop; that I may,
In your Temple, when I pray,
Kisse the Altar, and confess
Ther's in love, no bitterness.

37

AMONG thy Fancies, tell me this,
What is the thing we call a kisse?
I shall resolve ye, what it is.

It is a creature born and bred
Between the lips, (all cherrie-red,)
By love and warme desires fed,
And makes more soft the Bridall Bed.

It is an active flame, that flies,
First, to the babies of the eyes;
And charmes them there with lullabies;
And stils the Bride too, when she cries.

Then to the chin, the cheek, the eare,
It frisks, and flyes, now here, now there,
'Tis now farre off, and then tis nere;
And here, and there, and every where.

Ha's it a speaking virtue? Yes;
How speaks it, say? Do you but this,
Part your joyn'd lips, then speaks your kisse;
And this loves sweetest language is.

Has it a body? I, and wings
With thousand rare encolourings:
And as it flyes, it gently sings,
Love, honie yeelds; but never stings.

❧

UPON JULIA'S BREASTS

DISPLAY thy breasts, my Julia, there let me
Behold that circummortall purity:
Betweene whose glories, there my lips Ile lay,
Ravisht, in that faire Via Lactea.

UPON JULIA'S WASHING HER
SELF IN THE RIVER

How fierce was I, when I did see
My Julia wash her self in thee!
So Lillies thorough Christall look:
So purest pebbles in the brook:
As in the River Julia did,
Halfe with a Lawne of water hid,
Into thy streames my self I threw,
And strugling there, I kist thee too;
And more had done (it is confest)
Had not thy waves forbad the rest.

❧

WHAT KIND OF MISTRESSE
HE WOULD HAVE

BE the Mistresse of my choice,
Cleane in manners, cleere in voice:
Be she witty, more then wise;
Pure enough, though not Precise:
Be she shewing in her dresse,
Like a civill Wilderness;
That the curious may detect
Order in a sweet neglect:
Be she rowling in her eye,
Tempting all the passers by:
And each Ringlet of her haire,
An Enchantment, or a Snare,
For to catch the Lookers on;
But her self held fast by none.
Let her Lucrece all day be,
Thais in the night, to me.
Be she such, as neither will
Famish me, nor over-fill.

I co'd but see thee yesterday
  Stung by a fretfull Bee;
And I the Javelin suckt away,
  And heal'd the wound in thee.

A thousand thorns, and Bryars & Stings,
  I have in my poore Brest;
Yet ne'r can see that salve which brings
  My Passions any rest.

As Love shall helpe me, I admire
  How thou canst sit and smile,
To see me bleed, and not desire
  To stench the blood the while.

If thou compos'd of gentle mould
  Art so unkind to me;
What dismall Stories will be told
  Of those that cruell be?

❧

THE PRIMROSE

  Aske me why I send you here
This sweet Infanta of the yeere?
  Aske me why I send to you
This Primrose, thus bepearl'd with dew?
  I will whisper to your eares,
The sweets of Love are mixt with tears.

  Ask me why this flower do's show
So yellow-green, and sickly too?
  Ask me why the stalk is weak
And bending, (yet it doth not break?)
  I will answer, These discover
What fainting hopes are in a Lover.

HAVE ye beheld (with much delight)
A red-Rose peeping through a white?
Or else a Cherrie (double grac't)
Within a Lillie? Center plac't?
Or ever mark't the pretty beam,
A Strawberry shewes halfe drown'd in Creame?
Or seen rich Rubies blushing through
A pure smooth Pearle, and Orient too?
So like to this, nay all the rest,
Is each neate Niplet of her breast.

&

TO JULIA, IN HER DAWN,
OR DAY-BREAKE

By the next kindling of the day
 My Julia thou shalt see,
Ere Ave-Mary thou canst say
 Ile come and visit thee.

Yet ere thou counsel'st with thy Glasse,
 Appeare thou to mine eyes
As smooth, and nak't, as she that was
 The prime of Paradice.

If blush thou must, then blush thou through
 A Lawn, that thou mayst looke
As purest Pearles, or Pebles do
 When peeping through a Brooke.

As Lillies shrin'd in Christall, so
 Do thou to me appeare;
Or Damask Roses, when they grow
 To sweet acquaintance there.

41

UPON JULIA'S HAIRE, BUNDLED UP IN A GOLDEN NET

TELL me, what needs those rich deceits,
These golden Toyles, and Trammel-nets,
To take thine haires when they are knowne
Already tame, and all thine owne?
'Tis I am wild, and more then haires
Deserve these Meshes and those snares.
Set free thy Tresses, let them flow
As aires doe breathe, or winds doe blow:
And let such curious Net-works be
Lesse set for them, then spred for me.

❧

UPON HIS KINSWOMAN MISTRESSE BRIDGET HERRICK

SWEET Bridget blusht, & therewithall,
Fresh blossoms from her cheekes did fall.
I thought at first 'twas but a dream,
Till after I had handled them;
And smelt them, then they smelt to me,
As Blossomes of the Almond Tree.

❧

THE BRIDE-CAKE

THIS day my Julia thou must make
For Mistresse Bride, the wedding Cake:
Knead but the Dow and it will be
To paste of Almonds turn'd by thee:
Or kisse it thou, but once, or twice,
And for the Bride-Cake ther'l be Spice.

42

THOU art to all lost love the best,
　　The onely true plant found,
Wherewith young men and maids distrest,
　　And left of love, are crown'd.

When once the Lovers Rose is dead,
　　Or laid aside forlorne;
Then Willow-garlands, 'bout the head,
　　Bedew'd with teares, are worne.

When with Neglect, (the Lovers bane)
　　Poore Maids rewarded be,
For their love lost; their onely gaine
　　Is but a Wreathe from thee.

And underneath thy cooling shade,
　　(When weary of the light)
The love-spent Youth, and love-sick Maid,
　　Come to weep out the night.

❧

TO THE WATER NYMPHS
AT THE FOUNTAIN

REACH, with your whiter hands, to me,
　　Some Christall of the Spring;
And I, about the Cup shall see
　　Fresh Lillies flourishing.

Or else sweet Nimphs do you but this;
　　To'th' Glasse your lips encline;
And I shall see by that one kisse,
　　The Water turn'd to Wine.

Blessings, in abundance come,
To the Bride, and to her Groome;
May the Bed, and this short night,
Know the fulness of delight!
Pleasures, many here attend ye,
And ere long, a Boy Love send ye
Curld and comely, and so trimme,
Maides (in time) may ravish him.
Thus a dew of Graces fall
On ye both; Goodnight to all.

❧

UPON CUPID

Love, like a Beggar, came to me
  With Hose and Doublet torne:
His Shirt bedangling from his knee,
  With Hat and Shooes out-worne.

He askt an almes; I gave him bread,
  And meat too, for his need:
Of which, when he had fully fed,
  He wished me all Good speed.

Away he went, but as he turn'd
  (In faith I know not how)
He toucht me so, as that I burn,
  And am tormented now.

Love's silent flames, and fires obscure
  Then crept into my heart;
And though I saw no Bow, I'm sure,
  His finger was the dart.

I WILL confesse
With Cheerfulnesse,
That Love is a thing so likes me,
That let her lay
On me all day,
Ile kiss the hand that strikes me.

I will not, I,
Now blubb'ring, cry,
It (Ah!) too late repents me
That I did fall
To love at all,
Since love so much contents me.

No, no, Ile be
In fetters free;
While others they sit wringing
Their hands for paine;
Ile entertaine
The wounds of love with singing.

With Flowers and Wine,
And Cakes Divine,
To strike me I will tempt thee:
Which done; no more
Ile come before
Thee and thine Altars emptie.

A VOW TO VENUS

HAPPILY I had a sight
Of my dearest deare last night;
Make her this day smile on me,
And Ile Roses give to thee.

Lets call for Hymen if agreed thou art;
Delays in love but crucifie the heart.
Loves thornie Tapers yet neglected lye:
Speak thou the word, they'l kindle by and by.
The nimble howers wooe us on to wed,
And Genius waits to have us both to bed.
Behold, for us the Naked Graces stay
With maunds of roses for to strew the way:
Besides, the most religious Prophet stands
Ready to joyne, as well our hearts as hands.
Juno yet smiles; but if she chance to chide,
Ill luck 'twill bode to th' Bridegroome and the Bride.
Tell me Anthea, dost thou fondly dread
The loss of that we call a Maydenhead?
Come, Ile instruct thee. Know, the vestall fier
Is not by mariage quencht, but flames the higher.

THE SHOWRE OF BLOSSOMES

Love in a showre of Blossomes came
Down, and halfe drown'd me with the same:
The Blooms that fell were white and red;
But with such sweets commingled,
As whether (this) I cannot tell
My sight was pleas'd more, or my smell:
But true it was, as I rowl'd there,
Without a thought of hurt, or feare;
Love turn'd himselfe into a Bee,
And with his Javelin wounded me:
From which mishap this use I make,
Where most sweets are, there lyes a Snake.
Kisses and Favours are sweet things,
But Those have thorns, and These have stings.

TO DIANEME

GIVE me one kisse,
   And no more;
If so be, this
   Makes you poore;
To enrich you,
   Ile restore
For that one, two
   Thousand score.

THE HEAD-AKE

MY head doth ake,
O Sappho! take
   Thy fillit,
And bind the paine;
Or bring some bane
   To kill it.

But lesse that part,
Then my poore heart,
   Now is sick:
One kisse from thee
Will counsell be,
   And Physick.

TO OENONE

THOU sayest Loves Dart
Hath prickt thy heart;
And thou do'st languish too:
If one poore prick,
Can make thee sick,
Say, what wo'd many do?

DEW sate on Julia's haire,
    And spangled too,
Like Leaves that laden are
    With trembling Dew:
Or glitter'd to my sight,
    As when the Beames
Have their reflected light,
    Daunc't by the Streames.

❧

STOOL-BALL

AT Stool-ball, Lucia, let us play,
    For Sugar-cakes and Wine;
Or for a Tansie let us pay,
    The losse or thine, or mine.

If thou, my Deere, a winner be
    At trundling of the Ball,
The wager thou shalt have, and me,
    And my misfortunes all.

But if (my Sweetest) I shall get,
    Then I desire but this;
That likewise I may pay the Bet,
    And have for all a kisse.

❧

UPON HER FEET

HER pretty feet
Like snailes did creep
    A little out, and then,
As if they started at Bo-peep,
    Did soon draw in agen.

I DO not love to wed,
Though I do like to wooe;
And for a maidenhead
Ile beg, and buy it too.

Ile praise, and Ile approve
Those maids that never vary;
And fervently Ile love;
But yet I would not marry.

Ile hug, Ile kisse, Ile play,
And Cock-like Hens Ile tread:
And sport it any way,
But in the Bridall Bed:

For why? that man is poore,
Who hath but one of many;
But crown'd he is with store,
That single may have any.

Why then, say, what is he
(To freedome so unknown)
Who having two or three,
Will be content with one?

∾

TO ROSES IN JULIA'S BOSOME

ROSES, you can never die,
Since the place wherein ye lye,
Heat and moisture mixt are so,
As to make ye ever grow.

THE BEGGER

SHALL I a daily Begger be,
For loves sake asking almes of thee?
Still shall I crave, and never get
A hope of my desired bit?
Ah cruell maides! Ile goe my way,
Whereas (perchance) my fortunes may
Finde out a Threshold or a doore,
That may far sooner speed the poore:
Where thrice we knock, and none will heare,
Cold comfort still I'm sure lives there.

THE TYTHE. TO THE BRIDE

IF nine times you your Bride-groome kisse;
The tenth you know the Parsons is.
Pay then your Tythe; and doing thus,
Prove in your Bride-bed numerous.
If children you have ten, Sir John
Won't for his tenth part ask you one.

THE FROZEN HEART

I FREEZE, I freeze, and nothing dwels
In me but Snow, and ysicles.
For pitties sake give your advice,
To melt this snow, and thaw this ice;
I'l drink down Flames, but if so be
Nothing but love can supple me;
I'l rather keepe this frost, and snow,
Then to be thaw'd, or heated so.

FRESH CHEESE AND CREAM

WO'D yee have fresh Cheese and Cream?
Julia's Breast can give you them:
And if more; Each Nipple cries,
To your Cream, her's Strawberries.

❧

A SONG UPON SILVIA

FROM me my Silvia ranne away,
    And running therewithall;
A Primrose Banke did cross her way,
    And gave my Love a fall.

But trust me now I dare not say,
    What I by chance did see;
But such the Drap'ry did betray
    That fully ravisht me.

❧

TO HIS MISTRESS

HELPE me! helpe me! now I call
To my pretty Witchcrafts all:
Old I am, and cannot do
That, I was accustom'd to.
Bring your Magicks, Spels, and Charmes,
To enflesh my thighs, and armes:
Is there no way to beget
In my limbs their former heat?
Aeson had (as Poets faine)
Baths that made him young againe:
Find that Medicine (if you can)
For your drie-decrepid man:
Who would faine his strength renew,
Were it but to pleasure you.

THE RAINBOW: OR CURIOUS COVENANT

Mine eyes, like clouds, were drizling raine,
And as they thus did entertaine
The gentle Beams from Julia's sight
To mine eyes level'd opposite:
O Thing admir'd! there did appeare
A curious Rainbow smiling there;
Which was the Covenant, that she
No more wo'd drown mine eyes, or me.

TO SILVIA

Pardon my trespasse (Silvia) I confesse,
My kisse out-went the bounds of shamfastnesse:
None is discreet at all times; no, *not Jove
Himselfe, at one time, can be wise, and Love.*

THE PRESENT: OR, THE BAG OF THE BEE

Fly to my Mistresse, pretty pilfring Bee,
And say, thou bring'st this Hony-bag from me:
When on her lip, thou hast thy sweet dew plac't,
Mark, if her tongue, but slily, steale a taste.
If so, we live; if not, with mournfull humme,
Tole forth my death; next, to my buryall come.

LOVE ME LITTLE, LOVE ME LONG

You say, to me-wards your affection's strong;
Pray love me little, so you love me long.
Slowly goes farre: The meane is best: Desire
Grown violent, do's either die, or tire.

AMONG the Mirtles, as I walkt,
Love and my sighs thus intertalkt:
Tell me, said I, in deep distresse,
Where I may find my Shepardesse.
Thou foole, said Love, know'st thou not this?
In every thing that's sweet, she is.
In yond' Carnation goe and seek,
There thou shalt find her lip and cheek:
In that ennamel'd Pansie by,
There thou shalt have her curious eye:
In bloome of Peach, and Roses bud,
There waves the Streamer of her blood.
'Tis true, said I, and thereupon
I went to pluck them one by one,
To make of parts an union;
But on a sudden all were gone.
At which I stopt; Said Love, these be
The true resemblances of thee;
For as these flowers, thy joyes must die,
And in the turning of an eye;
And all thy hopes of her must wither,
Like those short sweets ere knit together.

❧

TO HIS DEARE VALENTINE, MRS.
MARGARET FALCONBRIGE

Now is your turne (my Dearest) to be set
A Jem in this eternall Coronet:
'Twas rich before; but since your Name is downe,
It sparkles now like Ariadne's Crowne.
Blaze by this Sphere for ever: Or this doe,
Let Me and It shine evermore by you.

ONE night i' th' yeare my dearest Beauties, come
And bring those dew-drink offerings to my Tomb.
When thence ye see my reverend Ghost to rise,
And there to lick th' effused sacrifice:
Though palenes be the Livery that I weare,
Looke ye not wan, or colourlesse for feare.
Trust me I will not hurt ye; or once shew
The least grim looke, or cast a frown on you:
Nor shall the Tapers when I'm there, burn blew.
This I may do (perhaps) as I glide by,
Cast on my Girles a glance, and loving eye:
Or fold mine armes, and sigh, because I've lost
The world so soon, and in it, you the most.
Then these, no feares more on your Fancies fall,
Though then I smile, and speake no words at all.

THE VISION

ME thought I saw (as I did dreame in bed)
A crawling Vine about Anacreon's head:
Flusht was his face; his haires with oyle did shine;
And as he spake, his mouth ranne ore with wine.
Tipled he was; and tipling lispt withall;
And lisping reeld, and reeling like to fall.
A young Enchantresse close by him did stand
Tapping his plump thighes with a mirtle wand:
She smil'd; he kist; and kissing, cull'd her too;
And being cup-shot, more he co'd not doe.
For which (me thought) in prittie anger she
Snatcht off his Crown, and gave the wreath to me:
Since when (me thinks) my braines about doe swim,
And I am wilde and wanton like to him.

IN THE DARKE NONE DAINTY

NIGHT hides our thefts; all faults then pardon'd be:
All are alike faire, when no spots we see.
Lais and Lucrece, in the night time are
Pleasing alike; alike both singular:
Jone, and my Lady have at that time one,
One and the selfe-same priz'd complexion.
Then please alike the Pewter and the Plate;
The chosen Rubie, and the Reprobate.

❧

TO ANTHEA LYING IN BED

So looks Anthea, when in bed she lyes,
Orecome, or halfe betray'd by Tiffanies:
Like to a Twi-light, or that simpring Dawn,
That Roses shew, when misted o're with Lawn.
Twilight is yet, till that her Lawnes give way;
Which done, that Dawne, turns then to perfect day.

❧

TO ANTHEA

Now is the time, when all the lights wax dim;
And thou (Anthea) must withdraw from him
Who was thy servant. Dearest, bury me
Under that Holy-oke, or Gospel-tree:
Where (though thou see'st not) thou may'st think upon
Me, when thou yeerly go'st Procession:
Or for mine honour, lay me in that Tombe
In which thy sacred Reliques shall have roome:
For my Embalming (Sweetest) there will be
No Spices wanting, when I'm laid by thee.

TO ELECTRA

SHALL I go to Love and tell,
Thou art all turn'd isicle?
Shall I say her Altars be
Disadorn'd, and scorn'd by thee?
O beware! in time submit;
Love has yet no wrathfull fit:
If her patience turns to ire,
Love is then consuming fire.

❧

TO ELECTRA

I DARE not ask a kisse;
    I dare not beg a smile;
Lest having that, or this,
    I might grow proud the while.

No, no, the utmost share
    Of my desire, shall be
Onely to kisse that Aire,
    That lately kissed thee.

❧

TO JULIA

HELP me, Julia, for to pray,
Mattens sing, or Mattens say:
This I know, the Fiend will fly
Far away, if thou beest by.
Bring the Holy-water hither;
Let us wash, and pray together:
When our Beads are thus united,
Then the Foe will fly affrighted.

HOW HIS SOULE CAME ENSNARED

My soule would one day goe and seeke
For Roses, and in Julia's cheeke,
A richess of those sweets she found,
(As in an other Rosamond.)
But gathering Roses as she was,
(Not knowing what would come to passe)
It chanst a ringlet of her haire,
Caught my poore soule, as in a snare:
Which ever since has been in thrall,
Yet freedome, shee enjoyes withall.

᠄᠄

UPON LUCIA

I ASKT my Lucia but a kisse;
And she with scorne deny'd me this:
Say then, how ill sho'd I have sped,
Had I then askt her Maidenhead?

᠄᠄

THE HOUR-GLASSE

That Houre-glasse, which there ye see
With Water fill'd, (Sirs, credit me)
The humour was, (as I have read)
But Lovers tears inchristalled,
Which, as they drop by drop doe passe
From th' upper to the under-glasse,
Do in a trickling manner tell,
(By many a watrie syllable)
That Lovers tears in life-time shed,
Do restless run when they are dead.

AH my *Anthea!* Must my heart still break?
(Love makes me write, what shame forbids to speak).
Give me a kisse, and to that kisse a score;
Then to that twenty, adde an hundred more:
A thousand to that hundred: so kisse on,
To make that million, and when that is done,
Let's kisse afresh, as when we first begun.
But yet, though Love likes well such Scenes as these,
There is an Act that will more fully please:
Kissing and glancing, soothing, all make way
But to the acting of this private Play:
Name it I would; but being blushing red,
The rest Ile speak, when we meet both in bed.

HIS PARTING FROM MRS. DOROTHY KENEDAY

WHEN I did goe from theee, I felt that smart,
Which Bodies do, when Souls from them depart.

Thou did'st not mind it; though thou then might'st see
Me turn'd to tears; yet did'st not weep for me.

'Tis true, I kist thee; but I co'd not heare
Thee spend a sigh, t'accompany my teare.

Me thought 'twas strange, that thou so hard sho'dst prove,
Whose heart, whose hand, whose ev'ry part spake love.

Prethee (lest Maids sho'd censure thee) but say
Thou shed'st one teare, when as I went away;

And that will please me somewhat: though I know,
And Love will swear't, my Dearest did not so.

UPON JULIA'S UNLACING HERSELF

TELL, if thou canst, (and truly) whence doth come
This Camphire, Storax, Spiknard, Galbanum:
These Musks, these Ambers, and those other smells
(Sweet as the Vestrie of the Oracles.)
Ile tell thee; while my Julia did unlace
Her silken bodies, but a breathing space:
The passive Aire such odour then assum'd,
As when to Jove Great Juno goes perfum'd.
Whose pure-Immortal body doth transmit
A scent, that fills both Heaven and Earth with it.

TO THE FEVER, NOT TO TROUBLE JULIA

TH'AST dar'd too farre; but Furie now forbeare
To give the least disturbance to her haire:

But lesse presume to lay a Plait upon
Her skins most smooth, and cleare expansion.

'Tis like a Lawnie-Firmament as yet
Quite dispossest of either fray, or fret.

Come thou not neere that Filmne so finely spred,
Where no one piece is yet unlevelled.

This if thou dost, woe to thee Furie, woe,
Ile send such Frost, such Haile, such Sleet, and Snow,

Such Flesh-quakes, Palsies, and such fears as shall
Dead thee to th' most, if not destroy thee all.

And thou a thousand thousand times shalt be
More shak't thy selfe, then she is scorch't by thee.

Nature, Wine, Mirth
Moralities, etc.

THE BAG OF THE BEE

ABOUT the sweet bag of a Bee,
  Two Cupids fell at odds;
And whose the pretty prize shu'd be,
  They vow'd to ask the Gods.

Which Venus hearing; thither came,
  And for their boldness stript them:
And taking thence from each his flame;
  With rods of Mirtle whipt them.

Which done, to still their wanton cries,
  When quiet grown sh'ad seen them,
She kist, and wip'd their dove-like eyes;
  And gave the Bag between them.

TO CHERRY-BLOSSOMES

YE may simper, blush, and smile,
And perfume the aire a while:
But (sweet things) ye must be gone;
Fruit, ye know, is comming on:
Then, ah! Then, where is your grace,
When as Cherries come in place?

SHUT not so soon; the dull-ey'd night
  Ha's not as yet begunne
To make a seisure on the light,
  Or to seale up the Sun.

No Marigolds yet closed are;
  No shadowes great appeare;
Nor doth the early Shepheards Starre
  Shine like a spangle here.

Stay but till my Julia close
  Her life-begetting eye;
And let the whole world then dispose
  It selfe to live or dye.

❤

TO VIOLETS

WELCOME Maids of Honour,
    You doe bring
    In the Spring;
And wait upon her.

She has Virgins many,
    Fresh and faire;
    Yet you are
More sweet then any.

Y'are the Maiden Posies,
    And so grac't,
    To be plac't,
'Fore Damask Roses.

Yet though thus respected,
    By and by
    Ye doe lie,
Poore Girles, neglected.

HOW ROSES CAME RED

Roses at first were white,
    Till they co'd not agree,
Whether my Sapho's breast,
    Or they more white sho'd be.

But being vanquisht quite,
    A blush their cheeks bespred;
Since which (beleeve the rest)
    The Roses first came red.

❧

HOW VIOLETS CAME BLEW

Love on a day (wise Poets tell)
    Some time in wrangling spent,
Whether the Violets sho'd excell,
    Or she, in sweetest scent.

But Venus having lost the day,
    Poore Girles, she fell on you
And beat ye so, (as some dare say)
    Her blowes did make ye blew.

❧

THE SUCCESSION OF THE FOURE
SWEET MONTHS

First, April, she with mellow showrs
Opens the way for early flowers;
Then after her comes smiling May
In a more rich and sweet array:
Next enters June, and brings us more
Jems, then those two, that went before:
Then (lastly) July comes, and she
More wealth brings in, then all those three.

THE SPELL

HOLY Water come and bring;
Cast in Salt, for seasoning:
Set the Brush for sprinkling:
Sacred Spittle bring ye hither;
Meale and it now mix together;
And a little Oyle to either:
Give the Tapers here their light,
Ring the Saints-Bell, to affright
Far from hence the evill Sp'rite.

❧

WHY FLOWERS CHANGE COLOUR

THESE fresh beauties (we can prove)
Once were Virgins sick of love,
Turn'd to Flowers. Still in some
Colours goe, and colours come.

❧

MRS. ELIZ. WHEELER, UNDER
THE NAME OF AMARILLIS

SWEET Amarillis, by a Spring's
Soft and soule-melting murmurings,
Slept; and thus sleeping, thither flew
A Robin-Red-brest; who at view,
Not seeing her at all to stir,
Brought leaves and mosse to cover her:
But while he, perking, there did prie
About the Arch of either eye;
The lid began to let out day;
At which poore Robin flew away:
And seeing her not dead, but all disleav'd,
He chirpt for joy, to see himself disceav'd.

63

GET up, get up for shame, the Blooming Morne
Upon her wings presents the god unshorne.
    See how Aurora throwes her faire
    Fresh-quilted colours through the aire:
    Get up, sweet Slug-a-bed, and see
    The Dew-bespangling Herbe and Tree.
Each Flower has wept, and bow'd toward the East,
Above an hour since; yet you not drest,
    Nay! not so much as out of bed?
    When all the Birds have Mattens seyd,
    And sung their thankfull Hymnes: 'tis sin,
    Nay, profanation to keep in,
When as a thousand Virgins on this day,
Spring, sooner then the Lark, to fetch in May.

Rise; and put on your Foliage, and be seene
To come forth, like the Spring-time, fresh and greene;
    And sweet as Flora. Take no care
    For Jewels for your Gowne, or Haire:
    Feare not; the leaves will strew
    Gemms in abundance upon you:
Besides, the childhood of the Day has kept,
Against you come, some Orient Pearls unwept:
    Come, and receive them while the light
    Hangs on the Dew-locks of the night:
    And Titan on the Eastern hill
    Retires himselfe, or else stands still
Till you come forth. Wash, dresse, be briefe in praying:
Few Beads are best, when once we goe a Maying.

Come, my Corinna, come; and comming, marke
How each field turns a street; each street a Parke
    Made green, and trimm'd with trees: see how

Devotion gives each House a Bough,
Or Branch: Each Porch, each doore, ere this,
An Arke a Tabernacle is
Made up of white-thorn neatly enterwove;
As if here were those cooler shades of love.
Can such delights be in the street,
And open fields, and we not see't?
Come, we'll abroad; and let's obay
The Proclamation made for May:
And sin no more, as we have done, by staying;
But my Corinna, come, let's goe a Maying.

There's not a budding Boy, or Girle, this day,
But is got up, and gone to bring in May.
A deale of Youth, ere this, is come
Back, and with White-thorn laden home.
Some have dispatcht their Cakes and Creame,
Before that we have left to dreame:
And some have wept, and woo'd, and plighted Troth,
And chose their Priest, ere we can cast off sloth:
Many a green-gown has been given;
Many a kisse, both odde and even:
Many a glance too has been sent
From out the eye, Loves Firmament:
Many a jest told of the Keyes betraying
This night, and Locks pickt, yet w'are not a Maying.

Come, let us goe, while we are in our prime;
And take the harmlesse follie of the time.
We shall grow old apace, and die
Before we know our liberty.
Our life is short; and our dayes run
As fast away as do's the Sunne:
And as a vapour, or a drop of raine

Once lost, can ne'r be found againe:
    So when or you or I are made
    A fable, song, or fleeting shade;
    All love, all liking, all delight
    Lies drown'd with us in endlesse night.
Then while time serves, and we are but decaying;
Come, my Corinna, come, let's goe a Maying.

⁓

HOW SPRINGS CAME FIRST

THESE Springs were Maidens once that lov'd,
But lost to that they most approv'd:
My Story tells, by Love they were
Turn'd to these Springs, which wee see here:
The pretty whimpering that they make,
When of the Banks their leave they take;
Tels ye but this, they are the same,
In nothing chang'd but in their name.

⁓

TO MARYGOLDS

GIVE way, and be ye ravisht by the Sun,
(And hang the head when as the Act is done)
Spread as He spreads; wax lesse as He do's wane;
And as He shuts, close up to Maids again.

⁓

HOW MARIGOLDS CAME YELLOW

JEALOUS Girles these sometimes were,
While they liv'd, or lasted here:
Turn'd to Flowers, still they be
Yellow, markt for Jealousie.

66

TO MEDDOWES

YE have been fresh and green,
　　Ye have been fill'd with flowers:
And ye the Walks have been
　　Where Maids have spent their houres.

You have beheld, how they
　　With Wicker Arks did come
To kisse, and beare away
　　The richer Couslips home.

Y'ave heard them sweetly sing,
　　And seen them in a Round:
Each Virgin, like a Spring,
　　With Hony-succles crown'd.

But now, we see, none here,
　　Whose silv'rie feet did tread,
And with dishevell'd Haire,
　　Adorn'd this smoother Mead.

Like Unthrifts, having spent,
　　Your stock, and needy grown,
Y'are left here to lament
　　Your poore estates, alone.

❧

A HYMNE TO BACCHUS

BACCHUS, let me drink no more;
Wild are Seas, that want a shore.
When our drinking has no stint,
There is no more pleasure in't.
I have drank up for to please
Thee, that great cup Hercules:
Urge no more; and there shall be
Daffadills g'en up to Thee.

TO SIR CLIPSEBY CREW

GIVE me wine, and give me meate,
To create in me a heate,
That my pulses high may beate.

Cold and hunger never yet
Co'd a noble Verse beget;
But your Boules with Sack repleat,

Give me these (my Knight) and try
In a Minutes space how I
Can runne mad, and Prophesie.

Then if any Peece proves new,
And rare, Ile say (my dearest Crew)
It was full enspir'd by you.

❧

TO A BED OF TULIPS

BRIGHT Tulips, we do know,
You had your comming hither;
And Fading-time do's show,
That Ye must quickly wither.

Your Sister-hoods may stay,
And smile here for your houre;
But dye ye must away:
Even as the Meanest Flower.

Come Virgins then, and see
Your frailties; and bemone ye;
For lost like these, 'twill be,
As Time had never known ye.

TO BACCHUS, A CANTICLE

WHITHER dost thou whorry me,
Bacchus, being full of Thee?
This way, that way, that way, this,
Here, and there a fresh Love is.
That doth like me, this doth please;
Thus a thousand Mistresses,
I have now; yet I alone,
Having All injoy not One.

THE COBLERS CATCH

COME sit we by the fires side;
   And roundly drinke we here;
Till that we see our cheekes Ale-dy'd
   And noses tann'd with Beere.

THE MAY-POLE

   THE May-pole is up,
   Now give me the cup;
I'l drink to the Garlands a-round it:
   But first unto those
   Whose hands did compose
The glory of flowers that crown'd it.

   A health to my Girles,
   Whose husbands may Earles
Or Lords be, (granting my wishes)
   And when that ye wed
   To the Bridall Bed,
Then multiply all, like to Fishes.

LET us now take time, and play,
Love, and live here while we may;
Drink rich wine; and make good cheere,
While we have our being here:
For, once dead, and laid i'th grave,
No return from thence we have.

CEREMONIES FOR CANDLEMASSE EVE

DOWN with the Rosemary and Bayes,
   Down with the Misleto;
In stead of Holly, now up-raise
   The greener Box (for show).

The Holly hitherto did sway;
   Let Box now domineere;
Untill the dancing Easter-day,
   Or Easters Eve appeare.

Then youthfull Box which now hath grace,
   Your houses to renew;
Grown old, surrender must his place,
   Unto the crisped Yew.

When Yew is out, then Birch comes in,
   And many Flowers beside;
Both of a fresh, and fragrant kinne
   To honour Whitsontide.

Green Rushes then, and sweetest Bents,
   With cooler Oken boughs;
Come in for comely ornaments,
   To re-adorn the house.
Thus times do shift; each thing his turne do's hold;
New things succeed, as former things grow old.

70

COME, bring with a noise,
My merrie merrie boyes,
The Christmas Log to the firing;
While my good Dame, she
Bids ye all be free;
And drink to your hearts desiring.

With the last yeeres brand
Light the new block, And
For good successe in his spending,
On your Psaltries play,
That sweet luck may
Come while the Log is a tending.

Drink now the strong Beere,
Cut the white loafe here,
The while the meat is a shredding;
For the rare Mince-Pie
And the Plums stand by
To fill the Paste that's a kneading.

❧

TO HIS MAID PREW

THESE Summer-Birds did with thy Master stay
The times of warmth; but then they flew away
Leaving their Poet (being now grown old)
Expos'd to all the comming Winters cold.
But thou kind Prew did'st with my Fates abide,
As well the Winters, as the Summers Tide:
For which thy Love, live with thy Master here,
Not two, but all the seasons of the yeare.

A LYRICK TO MIRTH

WHILE the milder Fates consent,
Let's enjoy our merryment:
Drink, and dance, and pipe, and play;
Kisse our Dollies night and day:
Crown'd with clusters of the Vine;
Let us sit, and quaffe our wine.

Call on Bacchus; chaunt his praise;
Shake the Thyrse, and bite the Bayes:
Rouze Anacreon from the dead;
And return him drunk to bed:
Sing o're Horace; for ere long
Death wil come and mar the song:

Then shall Wilson and Gotiere
Never sing, or play more here.

❧

A SONG TO THE MASKERS

COME down, and dance ye in the toyle
  Of pleasures, to a Heate;
But if to moisture, Let the oyle
  Of Roses be your sweat.

Not only to your selves assume
  These sweets, but let them fly;
From this, to that, and so Perfume
  E'ne all the standers by.

As Goddesse Isis (when she went,
  Or glided through the street)
Made all that touch't her with her scent,
  And whom she touch't, turne sweet,

72

TO M. KELLAM

WHAT can my Kellam drink his Sack
   In Goblets to the brim,
And see his Robin Herrick lack,
   Yet send no Boules to him?

For love or pitie to his Muse,
   (That she may flow in Verse)
Contemne to recommend a Cruse,
   But send to her a Tearce.

❦

A BACCHANALIAN VERSE

FILL me a mighty Bowle
   Up to the brim:
   That I may drink
Unto my Johnsons soule.

Crowne it agen agen;
   And thrice repeat
   That happy heat;
To drink to Thee my Ben.

Well I can quaffe, I see,
   To th' number five,
   Or nine; but thrive
In frenzie ne'r like thee.

❦

ON A PERFUM'D LADY

You say y'are sweet; how sho'd we know
Whether that you be sweet or no?
From Powders and Perfumes keep free;
Then we shall smell how sweet you be.

73

FAREWELL thou Thing, time-past so knowne, so deare
To me, as blood to life and spirit: Neare,
Nay, thou more neare then kindred, friend, man, wife,
Male to the female, soule to body: Life
To quick action, or the warme soft side
Of the resigning, yet resisting Bride.
The kisse of Virgins; First-fruits of the bed;
Soft speech, smooth touch, the lips, the Maiden-head:
These, and a thousand sweets, co'd never be
So neare, or deare, as thou wast once to me.
O thou the drink of Gods, and Angels! Wine
That scatter'st Spirit and Lust; whose purest shine,
More radiant then the Summers Sun-beams shows;
Each way illustrious, brave; and like to those
Comets we see by night; whose shagg'd portents
Fore-tell the comming of some dire events:
Or some full flame, which with a pride aspires,
Throwing about his wild, and active fires.
'Tis thou, above Nectar, O Divinest soule!
(Eternall in thy self) that canst controule
That, which subverts whole nature, grief and care;
Vexation of the mind, and damn'd Despaire.
'Tis thou, alone, who with thy Mistick Fan,
Work'st more then Wisdome, Art, or Nature can,
To rouze the sacred madnesse; and awake
The frost-bound blood, and spirits; and to make
Them frantick with thy raptures, flashing through
The soule, like lightning, and as active too.
'Tis not Apollo can, or those thrice three
Castalian Sisters, sing, if wanting thee.
Horace, Anacreon both had lost their fame,
Hadst thou not fill'd them with thy fire and flame.
Phoebean splendour! and thou Thespian spring!
Of which, sweet Swans must drink, before they sing

Their true-pac'd Numbers, and their Holy-Layes,
Which makes them worthy Cedar, and the Bayes.
But why? why longer doe I gaze upon
Thee with the eye of admiration?
Since I must leave thee; and enforc'd, must say
To all thy witching beauties, Goe, Away.
But if thy whimpring looks doe ask me why?
Then know, that Nature bids thee goe, not I.
'Tis her erroneous self has made a braine
Uncapable of such a Soveraigne,
As is thy powerful selfe. Prethee not smile;
Or smile more inly; lest thy looks beguile
My vowes denounc'd in zeale, which thus much show thee,
That I have sworn, but by thy looks to know thee.
Let others drink thee freely; and desire
Thee and their lips espous'd; while I admire,
And love thee; but not taste thee. Let my Muse
Faile of thy former helps; and onely use
Her inadult'rate strength: what's done by me
Hereafter, shall smell of the Lamp, not thee.

❧

THE WATCH

MAN is a Watch, wound up at first, but never
Wound up again: Once down, He's down for ever.
The Watch once downe, all motions then do cease;
And Mans Pulse stopt, *All Passions sleep in Peace.*

❧

UPON A SWEET VOICE

So long you did not sing, or touch your Lute,
We knew 'twas Flesh and Blood, that there sate mute.
But when your Playing, and your Voice came in,
'Twas no more you then, but a Cherubin.

75

FOUR THINGS MAKE US HAPPY

Health is the first good lent to men;
A gentle disposition then:
Next, to be rich by no by-wayes;
Lastly, with friends t'enjoy our dayes.

❧

FELICITY, QUICK OF FLIGHT

Every time seemes short to be,
That's measur'd by felicity:
But one halfe houre, that's made up here
With griefe; seemes longer then a yeare.

❧

TO BLOSSOMS

Faire pledges of a fruitfull Tree,
    Why do yee fall so fast?
    Your date is not so past;
But you may stay yet here a while,
To blush and gently smile;
    And go at last.

What, were yee borne to be
    An houre or half's delight;
    And so to bid goodnight?
'Twas pitie Nature brought yee forth
Meerly to shew your worth,
    And lose you quite.

But you are lovely Leaves, where we
    May read how soon things have
    Their end, though ne'r so brave:
And after they have shown their pride,
Like you a while: They glide
    Into the Grave.

No fault in women to refuse
The offer, which they most wo'd chuse.
No fault in women, to confesse
How tedious they are in their dresse.
No fault in women, to lay on
The tincture of Vermillion:
And there to give the cheek a die
Of white, where nature doth deny.
No fault in women, to make show
Of largeness, when th'are nothing so:
(When true it is, the out-side swels
With inward Buckram, little else.)
No fault in women, though they be
But seldome from suspition free:
No fault in womankind, at all,
If they but slip, and never fall.

UPON SOME WOMEN

Thou who wilt not love, doe this;
Learne of me what Woman is.

Something made of thred and thrumme;
A meere Botch of all and some.

Pieces, patches, ropes of haire;
In-laid Garbage ev'ry where.

Out-side silk, and out-side Lawne;
Sceanes to cheat us neatly drawne.

False in legs, and false in thighes;
False in breast, teeth, haire, and eyes:

False in head, and false enough;
Onely true in shreds and stuffe.

CONTENT, NOT CATES

'Tis not the food, but the content
That makes the Tables merriment.
Where Trouble serves the board, we eate
The Platters there, as soone as meat.
A little Pipkin with a bit
Of Mutton, or of Veale in it,
Set on my able, (Trouble-free)
More then a Feast contenteth me.

❧

HIS CAVALIER

Give me that man, that dares bestride
The active Sea-horse, and with pride,
Through that huge field of waters ride:
Who, with his looks too, can appease
The ruffling winds and raging Seas,
In mid'st of all their outrages.
This, this a virtuous man can doe,
Saile against Rocks, and split them too;
I! and a world of Pikes passe through.

❧

SAFETY TO LOOK TO ONE'S SELFE

For my neighbour Ile not know,
Whether high he builds or no:
Onely this Ile look upon,
Firm be my foundation.
Sound or unsound, let it be;
'Tis the lot ordain'd for me.
He who to the ground do's fall,
Has not whence to sink at all.

HIS DESIRE

GIVE me a man that is not dull,
When all the world with rifts is full:
But unamaz'd dares clearely sing,
When as the roof's a tottering:
And, though it falls, continues still
Tickling the Citterne with his quill.

MEN MIND NO STATE IN SICKNESSE

THAT flow of Gallants which approach
To kisse thy hand from out the coach;
That fleet of Lackeyes, which do run
Before thy swift Postilion;
Those strong-hoof'd Mules, which we behold,
Rein'd in with Purple, Pearl, and gold,
And shod with silver, prove to be
The drawers of the axeltree.
Thy Wife, thy Children, and the state
Of Persian Loomes, and antique Plate:
All these, and more, shall then afford
No joy to thee their sickly Lord.

TO MUSICK

BEGIN to charme, and as thou stroak'st mine
        eares
With thy enchantment, melt me into tears.
Then let thy active hand scu'd o're thy Lyre:
And make my spirits frantick with the fire.
That done, sink down into a silv'rie straine;
And make me smooth as Balme, and Oile
        againe.

Himself & His Book

A TERNARIE OF LITTLES, UPON A PIPKIN
OF JELLIE SENT TO A LADY

A LITTLE Saint best fits a little Shrine,
A little prop best fits a little Vine,
As my small Cruse best fits my little Wine.

A little Seed best fits a little Soyle,
A little Trade best fits a little Toyle:
As my small Jarre best fits my little Oyle.

A little Bin best fits a little Bread,
A little Garland fits a little Head:
As my small stuffe best fits my little Shed.

A little Hearth best fits a little Fire,
A little Chappell fits a little Quire,
As my small Bell best fits my little Spire.

A little streame best fits a little Boat;
A little lead best fits a little Float;
As my small Pipe best fits my little note.

A little meat best fits a little bellie,
As sweetly Lady, give me leave to tell ye
This little Pipkin fits this little Jellie.

80

ONELY a little more
    I have to write,
    Then Ile give o're,
And bid the world Good-night.

'Tis but a flying minute,
    That I must stay,
    Or linger in it;
And then I must away.

O time that cut'st down all!
    And scarce leav'st here
    Memoriall
Of any men that were.

How many lye forgot
    In Vaults beneath?
    And piece-meale rot
Without a fame in death?

Behold this living stone,
    I reare for me,
    Ne'r to be thrown
Downe, envious Time by thee.

Pillars let some set up,
    (If so they please)
    Here is my hope,
And my Pyramides.

TO CRITICKS

ILE write, because Ile give
You Criticks means to live:
For sho'd I not supply
The Cause, th'effect wo'd die.

CHARM me asleep, and melt me so
   With thy Delicious Numbers;
That being ravisht, hence I goe
   Away in easie slumbers.
     Ease my sick head,
     And make my bed,
Thou Power that canst sever
     From me this ill:
     And quickly still:
     Though thou not kill
      My Fever.

Thou sweetly canst convert the same
   From a consuming fire,
Into a gentle-licking flame,
   And make it thus expire.
     Then make me weep
     My paines asleep;
And give me such reposes,
     That I, poore I,
     May think, thereby,
     I live and die
      'Mongst Roses.

Fall on me like a silent dew,
   Or like those Maiden showrs,
Which, by the peepe of day, doe strew
   A Baptime o're the flowers.
     Melt, melt my paines,
     With thy soft straines;
That having ease me given,
     With full delight,
     I leave this light;
     And take my flight
      For Heaven.

CALL me no more,
  As heretofore,
The musick of a Feast;
  Since now (alas)
  The mirth, that was
In me, is dead or ceast.

  Before I went
  To banishment
Into the loathed West;
  I co'd rehearse
  A Lyrick verse,
And speak it with the best.

  But time (Ai me)
  Has laid, I see
My Organ fast asleep;
  And turn'd my voice
  Into the noise
Of those that sit and weep.

LYRICK FOR LEGACIES

GOLD I've none, for use or show,
Neither Silver to bestow
At my death; but thus much know,
That each Lyrick here shall be
Of my love a Legacie,
Left to all posterity.
Gentle friends, then doe but please,
To accept such coynes as these;
As my last Remembrances.

83

FROM the dull confines of the drooping West,
To see the day spring from the pregnant East,
Ravisht in spirit, I come, nay more, I flie
To thee, blest place of my Nativitie!
Thus, thus with hallowed foot I touch the ground,
With thousand blessings by thy Fortune crown'd.
O fruitfull Genius! that bestowest here
An everlasting plenty, yeere by yeere.
O Place! O People! Manners! fram'd to please
All Nations, Customes, Kindreds, Languages!
I am a free-born Roman; suffer then,
That I amongst you live a Citizen.
London my home is: though by hard fate sent
Into a long and irksome banishment;
Yet since cal'd back; henceforward let me be,
O native countrey, repossest by thee!
For, rather then I'le to the West return,
I'le beg of thee first here to have mine Urn.
Weak I am grown, and must in short time fall;
Give thou my sacred Reliques Buriall.

A REQUEST TO THE GRACES

PONDER my words, if so that any be
Known guilty here of incivility:
Let what is graceless, discompos'd, and rude,
With sweetness, smoothness, softness, be endu'd.
Teach it to blush, to curtsie, lisp, and shew
Demure, but yet, full of temptation too.
Numbers ne'r tickle, or but lightly please,
Unlesse they have some wanton carriages.
This if ye do, each Piece will here be good,
And gracefull made, by your neate Sisterhood.

TO HIS BOOKE

WHILE thou didst keep thy Candor undefil'd,
Deerly I lov'd thee; as my first-borne child:
But when I saw thee wantonly to roame
From house to house, and never stay at home;
I brake my bonds of Love, and bad thee goe,
Regardlesse whether well thou sped'st, or no.
On with thy fortunes then, what e're they be;
If good I'le smile, if bad I'le sigh for Thee.

❧

HIS LAST REQUEST TO JULIA

I HAVE been wanton, and too bold I feare,
To chafe o're much the Virgins cheek or eare:
Beg for my Pardon Julia; *He doth winne*
Grace with the Gods, who's sorry for his sinne.
That done, my Julia, dearest Julia, come,
And go with me to chuse my Buriall roome:
My Fates are ended; when thy Herrick dyes,
Claspe thou his Book, then close thou up his Eyes.

❧

THE CURSE. A SONG

GOE, perjur'd man; and if thou ere return
To see the small remainders in mine Urne:
When thou shalt laugh at my Religious dust;
And ask, Where's now the colour, forme and trust
Of Womans beauty? and with hand more rude
Rifle the Flowers which the Virgins strew'd:
Know, I have pray'd to Furie, that some wind
May blow my ashes up, and strike thee blind.

HIS PRAYER TO BEN. JOHNSON

WHEN I a Verse shall make,
Know I have praid thee,
For old Religions sake,
Saint Ben to aide me.

Make the way smooth for me,
When I, thy Herrick,
Honouring thee, on my knee
Offer my Lyrick.

Candles Ile give to thee,
And a new Altar;
And thou Saint Ben, shalt be
Writ in my Psalter.

❧

A HYMNE TO THE GRACES

WHEN I love, (as some have told,
Love I shall when I am old)
O ye Graces! Make me fit
For the welcoming of it.
Clean my Roomes, as Temples be,
T' entertain that Deity.
Give me words wherewith to wooe,
Suppling and successefull too:
Winning postures; and withall,
Manners each way musicall:
Sweetnesse to allay my sowre
And unsmooth behaviour.
For I know you have the skill
Vines to prune, though not to kill,
And of any wood ye see,
You can make a *Mercury*.

TO HIS BOOKE

MAKE haste away, and let one be
A friendly Patron unto thee:
Lest rapt from hence, I see thee lye
Torn for the use of Pasterie:
Or see thy injur'd Leaves serve well,
To make loose Gownes for Mackarell:
Or see the Grocers in a trice,
Make hoods of thee to serve out Spice.

NOT EVERY DAY FIT FOR VERSE

'TIS not ev'ry day, that I
Fitted am to prophesie:
No, but when the Spirit fils
The fantastick Pannicles:
Full of fier; then I write
As the Godhead doth indite.
Thus inrag'd, my lines are hurl'd,
Like the Sybells, through the world.
Look how next the holy fier
Either slakes, or doth retire;
So the Fancie cooles, till when
That brave Spirit comes agen.

ON HIMSELFE

BORNE I was to meet with Age,
And to walke Life's pilgrimage.
Much I know of Time is spent,
Tell I can't, what's Resident.
Howsoever, cares, adue;
Ile have nought to say to you:
But Ile spend my comming houres,
Drinking wine, & crown'd with flowres.

HERE down my wearyed limbs Ile lay;
My Pilgrims staffe; my weed of grey:
My Palmers hat; my Scallops shell;
My Crosse; my Cord; and all farewell.
For having now my journey done,
(Just at the setting of the Sun)
Here I have found a Chamber fit,
(God and good friends be thankt for it)
Where if I can a lodger be
A little while from Tramplers free;
At my up-rising next, I shall,
If not requite, yet thank ye all.
Meane while, the Holy-Rood hence fright
The fouler Fiend, and evill Spright,
From scaring you or yours this night.

THE DEPARTURE OF THE
GOOD DAEMON

WHAT can I do in Poetry,
Now the good Spirit's gone from me?
Why nothing now, but lonely sit,
And over-read what I have writ.

DIVINATION BY A DAFFADILL

WHEN a Daffadill I see,
Hanging down his head t'wards me;
Guesse I may, what I must be:
First, I shall decline my head;
Secondly, I shall be dead;
Lastly, safely buryed.

I CANNOT pipe as I was wont to do,
Broke is my Reed, hoarse is my singing too:
My wearied Oat Ile hang upon the Tree,
And give it to the Silvan Deitie.

TO HIS VERSES

WHAT will ye (my poor Orphans) do
When I must leave the World (and you)
Who'l give ye then a sheltring shed,
Or credit ye, when I am dead?
Who'l let ye by their fire sit?
Although ye have a stock of wit,
Already coin'd to pay for it.
I cannot tell; unlesse there be
Some Race of old humanitie
Left (of the large heart, and long hand)
Alive, as Noble Westmorland;
Or gallant Newark; which brave two
May fost'ring fathers be to you.
If not; expect to be no less
Ill us'd, then Babes left fatherless.

DISCONTENTS IN DEVON

MORE discontents I never had
　　Since I was born, then here;
Where I have been, and still am sad,
　　In this dull Devon-shire:
Yet justly too I must confesse;
　　I ne'r invented such
Ennobled numbers for the Presse,
　　Then where I loath'd so much.

89

THE PARCAE, OR, THREE
DAINTY DESTINIES

THREE lovely Sisters working were
   (As they were closely set)
Of soft and dainty Maiden-haire,
   A curious Armelet.
I smiling, ask'd them what they did?
   (Faire Destinies all three)
Who told me, they had drawn a thred
   Of Life, and 'twas for me.
They shew'd me then, how fine 'twas spun;
   And I reply'd thereto,
I care not how soone 'tis done,
   Or cut, if cut by you.

ON HIMSELFE

ASKE me, why I do not sing
To the tension of the string,
As I did, not long ago,
When my numbers full did flow?
Griefe (ay me!) hath struck my Lute,
And my tongue at one time mute.

AGE UNFIT FOR LOVE

MAIDENS tell me I am old;
Let me in my Glasse behold
Whether smooth or not I be,
Or if haire remaines to me.
Well, or be't or be't not so,
This for certainty I know;
Ill it fits old men to play,
When that Death bids come away.

AN HYMNE TO THE MUSES

HONOUR to you who sit!
Neere to the well of wit;
And drink your fill of it.

Glory and worship be!
To you sweet Maids (thrice three)
Who still inspire me.

And teach me how to sing
Unto the Lyrick string
My measures ravishing.

Then while I sing your praise,
My Priest-hood crown with bayes
Green, to the end of dayes.

UPON HIMSELFE BEING BURIED

LET me sleep this night away,
Till the Dawning of the day:
Then at th' opening of mine eyes,
I, and all the world shall rise.

ON HIMSELFE

I WILL no longer kiss,
I can no longer stay;
The way of all Flesh is,
That I must go this day:
Since longer I can't live,
My frolick Youths adieu;
My Lamp to you Ile give,
And all my troubles too.

THE OLIVE BRANCH

SADLY I walk't within the field,
To see what comfort it wo'd yeeld:
And as I went my private way,
An Olive-branch before me lay:
And seeing it, I made a stay.
And took it up, and view'd it; then
Kissing the Omen, said Amen:
Be, be it so, and let this be
A Divination unto me:
That in short time my woes shall cease;
And Love shall crown my end with Peace.

TO ANTHEA

ANTHEA I am going hence
With some small stock of innocence:
But yet those blessed gates I see
Withstanding entrance unto me.
To pray for me doe thou begin,
The Porter then will let me in.

TO PERENNA, A MISTRESSE

DEARE Perenna, prethee come,
And with Smallage dresse my Tomb:
Adde a Cypresse-sprig thereto,
With a teare; and so Adieu.

ON HIS BOOK

To read my Booke the Virgin shie
May blush, (while Brutus standeth by:)
But when He's gone, read through what's writ,
And never staine a cheeke for it.

TO PERILLA

AH my Perilla! do'st thou grieve to see
Me, day by day, to steale away from thee?
Age cals me hence, and my gray haires bid come,
And haste away to mine eternal home;
'Twill not be long (Perilla) after this,
That I must give thee the supremest kisse.
Dead when I am, first cast in salt, and bring
Part of the creame from that Religious Spring;
With which (Perilla) wash my hands and feet;
That done, then wind me in that very sheet
Which wrapt thy smooth limbs (when thou didst implore
The Gods protection, but the night before)
Follow me weeping to my Turfe, and there
Let fall a Primrose, and with it a teare:
Then lastly, let some weekly-strewings be
Devoted to the memory of me:
Then shall my Ghost not walk about, but keep
Still in the coole, and silent shades of sleep.

❧

ON HIMSELFE

WEEPE for the dead, for they have lost this light:
And weepe for me, lost in an endlesse night.
Or mourne, or make a Marble Verse for me,
Who writ for many. *Benedicite.*

❧

TO HIS MUSE

WERE I to give thee Baptime, I wo'd chuse
To Christen thee, the Bride, the Bashfull Muse,
Or Muse of Roses: since that name does fit
Best with those Virgin-Verses thou hast writ:
Which are so cleane, so chast, as none may feare
Cato the Censor, sho'd he scan each here.

TO HIS GIRLES

Wanton Wenches doe not bring
For my haires black colouring:
For my Locks (Girles) let 'em be
Gray or white, all's one to me.

TO HIS GIRLES WHO WOULD
HAVE HIM SPORTFULL

Alas I can't, for tell me how
Can I be gamesome (aged now)
Besides ye see me daily grow
Here Winter-like, to Frost and Snow.
And I ere long, my Girles, shall see
Ye quake for cold to looke on me.

UPON HIS VERSES

What off-spring other men have got,
The how, where, when, I question not.
These are the Children I have left;
Adopted some; none got by theft.
But all are toucht (like lawfull plate)
And no Verse illegitimate.

TO HIS TOMB-MAKER

Go I must; when I am gone,
Write but this upon my Stone;
Chaste I liv'd, without a wife,
That's the Story of my life.
Strewings need none, every flower
Is in this word, Batchelour.

TO HIS FRIEND, ON THE
UNTUNEABLE TIMES

PLAY I co'd once; but (gentle friend) you see
My harp hung up, here on the Willow tree.
Sing I co'd once; and bravely too enspire
(With luscious Numbers) my melodious Lyre.
Draw I co'd once (although not stocks or stones,
Amphion-like) men made of flesh and bones,
Whether I wo'd; but (ah!) I know not how,
I feele in me, this transmutation now.
Griefe, (my dear friend) has first my Harp unstrung;
Wither'd my hand, and palsie-struck my tongue.

❧

ON HIMSELFE

ILE sing no more, nor will I longer write
Of that sweet Lady, or that gallant Knight:
Ile sing no more of Frosts, Snowes, Dews and Showers;
No more of Groves, Meades, Springs, and wreaths
      of Flowers:
Ile write no more, nor will I tell or sing
Of Cupid, and his wittie cozening:
Ile sing no more of death, or shall the grave
No more my Dirges, and my Trentalls have.

❧

ON HIMSELFE

IL'E write no more of Love; but now repent
Of all those times that I in it have spent.
Ile write no more of life; but wish twas ended,
And that my dust was to the earth commended.

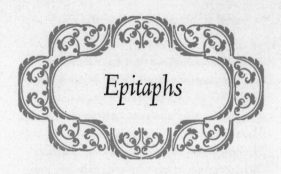

Epitaphs

UPON HIS KINSWOMAN MISTRIS
ELIZABETH HERRICK

Sweet virgin, that I do not set
The pillars up of weeping Jet,
Or mournfull Marble; let thy shade
Not wrathfull seem, or fright the Maide,
Who hither at her wonted howers
Shall come to strew thy earth with flowers.
No, know (Blest Maide) when there's not one
Remainder left of Brasse or stone,
Thy living Epitaph shall be,
Though lost in them, yet found in me.
Dear, in thy bed of Roses, then,
Till this world shall dissolve as men,
Sleep, while we hide thee from the light,
Drawing thy curtains round: Good night.

UPON HIS SPANIEL TRACIE

Now thou art dead, no eye shall ever see,
For shape and service, Spaniell like to thee.
This shall my love doe, give thy sad death one
Teare, that deserved of me a million.

LIFE of my life, take not so soone thy flight,
But stay the time till we have bade Good night.
Thou hast both Wind and Tide with thee; Thy way
As soone dispatcht is by the Night, as Day.
Let us not then so rudely henceforth goe
Till we have wept, kist, sigh't, shook hands, or so.
There's paine in parting; and a kind of hell,
When once true-lovers take their last Fare-well.
What? shall we too our endlesse leaves take here
Without a sad looke, or a solemne teare?
He knowes not Love, that hath not this truth proved,
Love is most loth to leave the thing beloved.
Pay we our Vowes, and goe; yet when we part,
Then, even then, I will bequeath my heart
Into thy loving hands: For Ile keep none
To warme my Breast, when thou my Pulse art gone.
No, here Ile last, and walk (a harmless shade)
About this Urne, wherein thy Dust is laid,
To guard it so, as nothing here shall be
Heavy, to hurt those sacred seeds of thee.

❧

UPON M. WILLIAM LAWES,
THE RARE MUSITIAN

SHO'D I not put on Blacks, when each one here
Comes with his Cypresse, and devotes a teare?
Sho'd I not grieve (my Lawes) when every Lute,
Violl, and Voice, is (by thy losse) struck mute?
Thy loss brave man! whose Numbers have been hurl'd,
And no less prais'd, then spread throughout the world.
Some have Thee call'd Amphion; some of us,
Nam'd thee Terpander, or sweet Orpheus:
Some this, some that, but all in this agree,
Musique had both her birth, and death with Thee.

AFTER the rare Arch-Poet JOHNSON dy'd,
The Sock grew loathsome, and the Buskins pride,
Together with the Stages glory stood
Each like a poore and pitied widowhood.
The Cirque prophan'd was; and all postures rackt:
For men did strut, and stride, and stare, not act.
Then temper flew from words; and men did squeake,
Looke red, and blow, and bluster, but not speake:
No Holy-Rage, or frantick-fires did stirre,
Or flash about the spacious Theater.
No clap of hands, or shout, or praises-proofe
Did crack the Play-house sides, or cleave her roofe.
Artlesse the Sceane was, and that monstrous sin
Of deep and *arrant ignorance* came in;
Such ignorance as theirs was, who once hist
At thy unequal'd Play, the Alchymist:
Oh fie upon 'em! Lastly too, all witt
In utter darkenes hid, and still will sit
Sleeping the lucklesse Age out, till that she
Her Resurrection ha's again with Thee.

UPON PREW HIS MAID

IN this little Urne is laid
Prewdence Baldwin (once my maid)
From whose happy spark here let
Spring the purple Violet.

UPON A MOTHER OF MANY CHILDREN

LET all chaste Matrons when they chance to see
My num'rous issue: Praise, and pitty me.
Praise me, for having such a fruitfull wombe;
Pity me too, who found so soone a Tomb.

TO THE REVEREND SHADE OF HIS
RELIGIOUS FATHER

THAT for seven Lusters I did never come
To doe the Rites to thy Religious Tombe:
That neither haire was cut, or true teares shed
By me, o'r thee, *(as justments to the dead)*
Forgive, forgive me; since I did not know
Whether thy bones had here their Rest, or no.
But now 'tis known, Behold; behold, I bring
Unto thy Ghost, th' Effused Offering:
And look, what Smallage, Night-shade, Cypresse, Yew,
Unto the shades have been, or now are due,
Here I devote; And something more then so;
I come to pay a Debt of Birth I owe.
Thou gav'st me life, (but Mortall;) For that one
Favour, Ile make full satisfaction;
For my life mortall, Rise from out thy Herse,
And take a life immortall from my Verse.

TO ROBIN RED-BREAST

LAID out for dead, let thy last kindnesse be
With leaves and mosse-work for to cover me:
And while the Wood-nimphs my old corps inter,
Sing thou my Dirge, sweet-warbling Chorister!
For Epitaph, in Foliage, next write this,
Here, here the tomb of Robin Herrick is.

UPON HIS SISTER-IN-LAW, MISTRESSE
ELIZAB: HERRICK

FIRST, for Effusions due unto the dead,
My solemne Vowes have here accomplished:
Next, how I love thee, that my griefe must tell,
Wherein thou liv'st for ever. Deare farewell.

UPON A CHILD THAT DYED

HERE she lies, a pretty bud,
Lately made of flesh and blood:

Who, as soone, fell fast asleep,
As her little eyes did peep.

Give her strewings; but not stir
The earth, that lightly covers her.

❧

UPON A LADY THAT DYED
IN CHILD-BED

As Gilly flowers do but stay
To blow, and seed, and so away;
So you sweet Lady (sweet as May)
The gardens-glory liv'd a while,
To lend the world your scent and smile.
But when your own faire print was set
Once in a Virgin Flosculet,
(Sweet as your selfe, and newly blown)
To give that life, resign'd your own:
But so, as still the mothers power
Lives in the pretty Lady-flower.

❧

AN EPITAPH UPON A CHILD

VIRGINS promis'd when I dy'd,
That they wo'd each Primrose-tide,

Duely, Morne and Ev'ning, come,
And with flowers dresse my Tomb.

Having promis'd, pay your debts,
Maids, and here strew Violets.

UPON A WIFE THAT DYED
MAD WITH JEALOUSIE

IN this little Vault she lyes,
Here, with all her jealousies:
Quiet yet; but if ye make
Any noise, they both will wake,
And such spirits raise, 'twill then
Trouble Death to lay agen.

❧

UPON A CHILD

HERE a pretty Baby lies
Sung asleep with Lullabies:
Pray be silent, and not stirre
Th' easie earth that covers her.

❧

ON HIMSELFE

I FEARE no Earthly Powers;
But care for crowns of flowers:
And love to have my Beard
With Wine and Oile besmear'd.
This day Ile drowne all sorrow;
Who knowes to live to morrow?

❧

TO HIS BOOK'S END
THIS LAST LINE HE'D HAVE PLAC'T:
JOCUND HIS MUSE WAS;
BUT HIS LIFE WAS CHASTE.

AN INDEX OF FIRST LINES

103

The End

THIS TEXT HAS BEENE
SETTE IN THE ESTIENNE TYPES,
& PRYNTED ON PAPER
MADE ESPECIALLIE FOR
THE PETER PAUPER PRESSE